D0111239

i wish
someone
had told me!

financial lessons
learned the hard way

Charlotte
S T A L L I N G S

I Wish Someone Had Told Me:
Financial Lessons Learned the Hard Way

© 2012, Charlotte Stallings

Registered with the Library of Congress

ISBN 0-9772084-0-0

Interior Book Design: Derick Brown
Cover Design: Derick Brown
Publisher: Getting $mart Books

Printed in the United States of America

i wish someone had told me!

dedication

To my wonderful and beautiful mother, Virgie McGregor, for praying God's favor over us long before it was popular, and for making her kids the center of her world.

To my super supportive husband, Ron, who encourages me to "Hit 50!" every day, and who has sustained and maintained so that I can pursue my dreams. Thank you! I love you and I appreciate all that you do to make life great for us.

To our Princess, Milan, who is a fabulous daughter, an awesome student, and a fierce, self-taught swimmer. I pinch myself everyday as a reminder of the wonderful privilege to be your mom.

To my brothers and sisters: James, Ruth, Ahmil and Ivy, thanks for enduring my "Thelma" years. You're the best siblings on the planet. And to my dad, James Sr. and my aunts, Effie Evans, Bernice Gilliard, and Debra Scott, you had a hand in helping shape who I am today. I love and appreciate you.

To all of my wonderful extended family, near and far, and especially my nieces and nephews, you make me proud to be Aunt Charlotte. Keep making big things happen each and every day.

i wish someone had told me!

acknowledgements

To Gracie White, aka Miss Hunter, thanks for making me memorize that Black History Month monologue. You saw something in me that I didn't know I possessed, and you lit a spark in me that continues to burn today.

To Hazel Birth, thank you for taking me on the trip to Lincoln University. You gave me the experience of college life for a weekend, which opened my mind to the possibilities that existed outside North Minneapolis.

Thanks to my sister-friends: Shirley Brown, Phyllis Sloan, Dr. Cheryl Crowell, Marilyn Wood, Pamela Miller, Janie Westbrook, Lisa Cunningham, Joyce Hayden, Laverne Stallings, Julie Gionet, Michelle Lloyd, Debra Hartsfield, Amber Lewing, Julie Goudeau, Jan Meriweather Davis, Terry Theall, Jacqui Goudeau, Shawn Hill, Victoria Ochiche, Angela Celestine, Dr. Gena Jerkins, Nikki Shaw, Henrenetta Denman, Kaye Flewellen, Charlene Hill, Mary Ayodele, Margo Hickman, Cecelia Fuller and Kim Richardson. You women have poured into me, laughed and cried with me, propped me up and walked along side me through whatever phase of life I was experiencing at the time. I love you!

To Bishop Shelton Bady, your support, encouragement, prayers and model of excellence have helped me navigate through life and business pursuits. Thank you!

To Laura Baker, Sam Horn, Sue Howard, Rosalind Hamilton and Derick Brown for being great resources in moving this book project forward even when I stalled out.

To Donna McMillan and Sedric Malone for your consistent inquiries about this book. I needed and appreciated your prodding.

And to every person who's sat in an audience and listened to me speak. You are the reason I do what I do!

contents

i wish someone had told me!

foreword

I certainly can identify with the title of this book - for many reasons, not the least of which is that it applies to my life. I remember coming out of college, getting my first job and just as quickly the taste of real debt. It wasn't long before I learned the truth of my parent's constant reminder, "Boy money doesn't grow on trees!" My solution to the problem seemed simple at the time – *just make more money!* I wish someone had told me how far off the mark I was.

For me, making more money meant becoming a professional athlete for 12 years in the National Football League (NFL). I thought this would solve all of my financial woes. What I didn't realize was that I was making the same errors in how I approached money, and if I didn't change my approach I would wind up making the same mistakes no matter how much money I made.

I was young, dumb and excited, playing pro ball, with a new wife and family, a big house, cars, parties and I thought it would never end. I fooled myself into thinking I'd start learning to manage my finances later, then later came and my NFL career was over and I had very little to show for it.

After football, I became a financial consultant, a partner in a small independent firm in Minneapolis. I was preaching some of the things Charlotte writes about but not practicing it, until my own finances spiraled out of control. Only then did I look in the mirror and say, 'It's time to make a change". Sooner or later life will force you to learn a few of the lessons Charlotte points out in this book.

The words financial planning, investments or portfolios can make people shudder and get nervous depending on their background, training, exposure or experience. Charlotte has written with this fact in mind, crafting a work that is relatable and easy to understand for everyone. Charlotte is my friend; an exceptional person who understands how to manage finances, but more importantly she knows how finances fit into the overall picture of life.

You won't find gimmicks or quick fixes between these pages, but rather a deeper understanding of fundamentally sound, proven approaches to take control of your financial future. Whether you are a successful businessperson, starting out on your own, or maybe even starting over in life, there is something in "I Wish Someone Had Told Me" just for *you*.

Greg Coleman
Minnesota Vikings, Sideline Analyst
Former Minnesota Vikings Player

introduction

I'm admitting that early on in my life, I was clueless when it came to building wealth. Like many people, I knew how to work and make money, and for the most part, that was the extent of my understanding of money management. I didn't know how to grow it, and I sure didn't know how to keep it.

After growing up in a single-parent home in North Minneapolis, I went to college and got a series of good jobs. I had a 401K...*and* I had a bunch of credit cards too! Basically, I lived in happy oblivion for a number of years racking up credit card debt, spending to escape or relieve stress and, of course, living beyond my means. The biggest eye opening time for me came when I started working for American Express Financial Advisors, (now Ameriprise Financial). In this position, I helped create marketing materials that explained investment strategies to clients. I'd sit at my desk, staring at my computer thinking, "I'm in debt up to my eyeballs, how can I help others?"

I have to smile when I think about it now, but what transformed my money consciousness was just a simple brochure that I picked up for research purposes. When I opened it, I saw a chart showing how much $100.00

invested once a month could earn over a 25-year period. There it was in black and white: money can grow significantly if one simply makes a point of consistently saving it, a little at a time. It's called dollar-cost-averaging and I loved it because it was easy to understand and easy to do!

Another thing in the brochure that caught my eye was that the people in it were ordinary people. These regular, everyday folks were accumulating wealth. Wealth, I then realized, was within everyone's grasp. When I was growing up, I thought that only certain people had wealth and that most of them were born into it. Wealth was out of reach for people like me, I reasoned. As my perspective broadened and my consciousness changed, so did my spending and saving habits.

Today I am more grounded because of the lessons I learned (sometimes the hard way) about restraint, resourcefulness, patience and imagination. These are the qualities I had to learn to draw upon to navigate my way through life and money. I learned so many money lessons the hard way! I *do* wish that someone had told me just a few of the tips in this book. That is why I am sharing them with you and why I hope you will share them with those you know.

Each chapter describes a different money-related dilemma that I, or people I've met and know, created through bad behavior or misunderstanding. (All names have been changed to protect the innocent…..and/or the guilty!) Following the dilemma is a *Lesson* to take away, and then the chapter closes with a *Refresh*. The *Refresh* offers you an idea or two on how to address this type of dilemma so you won't utter the words, "I wish someone had told me."

Remember, common sense has a way of becoming common culture. One by one, with careful spending and saving habits, we can all stand on firm financial ground with a cash reserve in one hand, and the ability to buy and experience the things we dream of in the other hand.   Prosperity is about so much more than a big bank account, rather it is about financial freedom, which is one of the first steps toward achieving your dreams in all areas of your life. And financial freedom, my friend, is my wish for you! ◆

Section I
examine where you are financially

chapter 1
money talk is good talk

Some topics are taboo in the course of general conversations, such as politics, religion, and yes… money. These topics can be off limits because they trigger deep-seated emotions, which generally are tied to upbringing, backgrounds and experiences. I don't know about the first two, but I can tell you that the more you make all aspects of money an openly discussed subject in your life, the better off you will be.

My first memories of money conversations go back to when I was in 6th grade. I thought it was cool when I got to stay up late on some weeknights with my mother after my brothers and sisters were asleep. It was during these late night snack sessions when my mom showed me how she juggled earnings from her bank job to make ends meet. We'd talk about school and the neighborhood news while munching on cookies, and then she'd start opening envelopes and pulling out these little pre-folded pages that had numbers printed all over them. She'd say, "Charlotte, this is the light bill. Right here (while pointing at numbers and circling them with her pen) it shows how much is due, but we don't have enough to pay it all this time, so we'll send them a check for this much." Sometimes she'd even let me write out the check, stuff it into the return envelope, seal it shut and put the stamp in the corner. It was during these times that I felt really grown-up and really money-smart.

So I was introduced to bills, how to pay those bills and stretching a dollar at a young age, and I was good at juggling money to meet expenses because my mother had taught me well. But we never really talked *strategically* about money, or the importance of saving and growing it for the long-term. It's not that saving wasn't important, but after the bills were paid, there wasn't too much money left over, and consequently there wasn't too much to talk about either.

Since then, I found out we weren't alone. I thought we didn't talk about money because we didn't have much of it, but I've discovered that middle class and affluent families also didn't talk about money. Several years ago I had the honor and privilege of meeting and working with Barbara Stanny, the author of *Prince Charming Isn't Coming*. Barbara's father and uncle founded H&R Block. She grew up wealthy and in a home where there was an abundance of financial knowledge, yet the topic of money was not commonplace around their dinner table. When later in life she found herself as a divorced, single parent with zero in her trust fund, she had to start talking about (*and* learning about) money in order to make a living.

The more you make all aspects of money an openly discussed subject in your life, the better off you will be.

So why is talking about money, among family or friends, so difficult? Could it be that money conversations can disrupt family harmony? A recent T. Rowe Price survey discovered that parents find it easier to talk to their kids about drugs and alcohol than about the family finances. Could it be that money talks can cast a light on our spending habits, which showcase our financial progress and successes, or those sometimes embarrassing financial failures. "In our culture, money and work are closely tied to our identities," says Dalton Conley, Ph.D., dean of social sciences at New York University. "Money conversations have a distinct moral tinge to them, which makes people uncomfortable." Let's face it, even the most general, innocent money comment can put us on the defensive and make us feel judged or awkward for all sorts of reasons.

As an adult I have come to understand the importance of integrating conversations about money, no matter how uncomfortable, into your life on a regular basis. Among other things, financial conversations teach important lessons about saving and goal setting. When my girlfriend Carolyn and her husband decided to open an art gallery together, they talked about their goals and they set up a budget. Together, they agreed to forego extras, like fancier cell phones or luxury vacations, to meet expenses. By talking openly and committing to honest, timely communication, they made their budget – and their business – work.

I can hear you saying, "But Charlotte, this isn't an easy thing to do!" Trust me, I feel you 100%. The task of talking about money hasn't been easy for me, and even today it can be tough. **I wish someone had told me** that talking about money is an open, healthy, and important part of family life. ◆

lesson

Whether you have a lot of money or a little, discuss it. Talk to your spouse, your roommate, your children – whoever is a part of your household. Talk about why you need it, what you're planning to use it for, and how you're going to use it to save or pay off debt. You can even talk about what you don't need or want. Just talk about money!

hit refresh

Here are some suggestions that will help you integrate the subject of money into daily conversations. Doing so will make the mechanics of your financial decisions open for inspection, and discussion, in your family.

Take Time for Money Huddles

Money Huddles are scheduled, designated times (weekly or monthly) when you meet with your spouse, roommate(s), or entire household to specifically discuss money. They are just as important as a business meeting you might have with your boss at work. They are most effective if the discussion focuses on budgets and planning instead of criticizing, blaming or judging. This is the time to be clear. Talk about your current spending, existing debt and anticipated expenses. Review any areas that are challenging or need review.

It's also important during the huddle to celebrate your wins and successes. These 'wins' can include things like:

- Only buying two coffees, this week, instead of six.
- Taking your lunch to work everyday.
- Paying off a delinquent account.

- Making a big dent on a credit card balance.
- Depositing overtime pay into your savings instead of spending it.

Setting time aside to discuss money allows you to honor your agreements and to communicate without being rushed or distracted.

The Big Family Purchase

The next time your family sits down for a meal together, have a conversation about a significant purchase you've got planned in the future. Start with this statement, "I know that we need a new_____. That costs about x dollars, I think that if we save x amount for x weeks or months, we should be able to afford it. What does everyone think about that?"

Vacation Plans

Or how about the family vacation you're planning. "We've been talking about taking a vacation for awhile, let's do it in June. Now let's go around the table and everybody give a couple ideas for ways that we can start saving now to be able to pay for it."

The Money Jar

Put an empty jar or container in the kitchen or family room where it's visible to everyone. At the end of every day, family members empty change from their wallets and pockets and put it into the jar. At mealtime, have discussions about what the family should do with all the money saved in the jar when it's filled up.

talk to me...

Is your family talking about money openly?

What tips do you have to help people open up with each other about their financial realities?

I'd love to hear your thoughts!

@CharStallings
facebook.com/iwishbook

chapter 2
review your credit report often

When I got married, I found the same 'money talks don't happen here' pattern from my childhood was also the prevailing thinking in my new home. My husband and I had adopted a 'don't ask, don't tell policy' about money at our house long before the U.S. military instituted theirs years ago.

For many people, avoiding the money topic also means avoiding a regular review of their credit report. Unfortunately that was the case for me and my husband, but we were about to learn an important lesson back then.

We were buying our first house, and we needed to get approval for a mortgage. When we sat down to review our reports we found a mountain of data, much of it concerning our past credit activity. I was amazed to see that my information went all the way back to when I was 16 and opened my first department store account. We had to go through years of detailed information with a fine-toothed comb. The experience was both anxiety-producing and enlightening.

To my surprise, I found historical issues that had been resolved but never removed. And the mistakes were wide ranging, for example, one of my brother's credit information was on my reports because our names were so similar. (The first five letters of our first name, our middle initial and last names were identical.)

To finally get approved, we had to explain in writing every negative entry on our credit reports. Had we not gone through that process, who knows what shape we'd be in today. At the time, credit reports were totally foreign to me. I had never reviewed my credit report nor did I know how it affected me.

I wish someone had told me when I was younger that my borrowing history would be put into a report that for years to come would affect my borrowing power and the interest rates that I could expect to pay. ◆

 lesson

Until you become familiar with your credit report and the data that paints your financial picture, you won't know what information is reported to lenders, and that information is vital for you to manage your money well. And when you see your credit report, it will bring home to you how important it is to make payments on time, dispute inaccurate entries and understand the pulse of your credit information. Ignoring your credit report won't make the information go away.

hit refresh

With identity theft and fraud so rampant today, it's even more crucial to review your credit report regularly. It's a law in the U.S. that everyone can get a free copy of their credit report once every 12 months from all three reporting agencies. This is true whether you've been turned down for credit or not.

Here is a good rule of thumb or pattern to follow: request your free reports from each reporting agency on a rolling basis (once every three or four months). Here's a simple schedule you can follow.

Time Period:	Download free credit report from:
January – April	Experion
May - August	Transunion
September - December	Equifax

Remember to visit www.annualcreditreport.com, the approved main portal, to download free copies of your credit reports. Doing a review several times a year puts you in the driver's seat, and allows you to compare and contrast information being collected on you from the three agencies. Your creditors may base their decisions on just one agency's information, so it benefits you to know what's there

Speaking of "knowing what's there", the president of the Houston Better Business Bureau (BBB) pointed out to me that you should also periodically review copies of your kids' credit reports. I imagine you're thinking, "But they're too young to have credit!" And that's exactly the point – the hackers and bad people know this. There are actual reported cases of fraudulent credit activity on the credit reports of minor children. Grab your kids' social security numbers and sit down at your nearest computer to get started.

Finally, your FICO (Fair Isaac Company) score is a number creditors use to assess your credit worthiness. The higher the FICO score, the better. If your number is lower, it doesn't mean you cannot get credit, it simply means you may not get the best terms or rates. This is a good piece of information for you to know also. You can learn what your FICO score is by visiting www.myfico.com and please note that there may be a nominal fee for this information.

For help in understanding your report and resolving problems, visit Money Management International's website at www.moneymanagement.org.

talk to me...

When is the last time you pulled your credit report? What were your thoughts when you saw all the information there? Have you struggled with simply looking at the reports because they're so overwhelming?

Write me and tell me about your experiences with this important and powerful document.

I'd like to know!

@CharStallings
facebook.com/iwishbook

chapter 3
the jones' don't care

Do you know anyone who doesn't just want to keep up with the Jones', but their goal is to obliterate them? Maybe they have to be the first person on the block (or in the office) to have the latest gadget or tech toy loaded with apps that they'll never understand or use. Or they buy the newest cell phone at full price even though their current one is less than six months old. Maybe they wouldn't be caught dead (even in the grocery store) dressed in anything but designer threads from head-to-toe, or they change cars like they change clothes – which is often.

"No Charlotte, I don't know anyone like this, in fact this sounds kind of exaggerated and extreme if you ask me." Extreme? Maybe. Real-world? Absolutely! The truth is many people live their lives this way. In their hearts and minds they say, "Look at me! I've got it! I'm the best! I'm first to have it!" But sadly, if you follow them to the bank, being first and best, has caused them to be broke and busted.

Keeping up with the Jones' is common for those of us (yes, me too…been there; done that) who struggle with an affliction I call the *desire mentality*. We spend lots of time standing on the outside-looking-in at people who seem to have it all, not realizing that the Jones' have their own issues and challenges and really don't care whether you keep up with them or not! If your motivation is to keep up with others rather than keeping your goals in front of you, you likely won't be successful at either.

Comparing ourselves to others can be financial sabotage and the culprit behind a lot of unnecessary debt and wasteful purchasing. Instead, compare yourself to how close you are to achieving *your own* personal financial goals. **I wish someone had told me** to focus on my own goals and not my neighbor's, or co-worker's, or friend's lifestyle.

So how does this *desire mentality* find its way into our lives?

If your motivation is to keep up with others rather than keeping your goals in front of you, you likely won't be successful

Raise your hand if you agree that in our world today it is incredibly easy to get sucked into living beyond our means. If you have both hands high in the air, you and I are on the same page. Do me a favor - take a few minutes to think about, and list, all of the ways you can be lured into spending more and more of your hard-earned paycheck each month.

What did you come up with? When I made my list, I realized that there can be a strong external pull through the efforts of skillful marketers. Product manufacturers wear us down with non-stop television commercials and pop-up ads on our computers, tablets and cell phones that tout all kinds of things, like….

- New car models rolling out every year.
- New styles, colors and fashion trends that leap off magazine covers

every season.

- Glitzy new technology and games launched several times a year (and we wait in line for hours to buy them).
- New Jordan's released almost monthly it seems.
- And those blasted Groupon and Living Social deals that cram our inboxes all day, every day!

But not so quick! We can't blame it all on marketing, we play a part in this too. Have you ever rationalized and said, "I work really hard, I deserve to have this. Heck, I've earned it and I'm going to get it!" That my friend is the exact kind of internal dialogue that nurtures and fans the flames of a *desire mentality*.

My girlfriend, Monica, is married to a man who lives in the "now and today," and while he's taught her to live more in the present, his excessive, gotta-have-it-right-now, "The fellas are gonna like this," spending has, on several occasions, delayed and prevented them from reaching their goals. For instance, after deciding to save for a trip overseas, Monica says that her husband drove up to the house one afternoon in a new car that he decided in the space of 20 minutes to buy. I'll let you imagine her reaction.

When you pay for something because of pride, appearance or an insatiable desire, ask yourself, "What am I taking away from to pay for this?" It could be your retirement savings, education for your kids, your mortgage, or that dream vacation. You could also be taking away precious time from your family because you're working more to make up the difference. **I wish someone had told me** that living within my means is a good thing.

Eventually Monica and her husband realized that not only were they not saving, they were in the red every month because they were living beyond their means. They came to me for advice and I sent them to a professional debt counselor. I know Monica well and it took a lot for her *and* her husband to admit that they were struggling. But acknowledgement of a problem is the first step in turning things around…and that's what they did. ◆

lesson

If you continue to feed into the desire mentality mindset, you won't get where you want to be; instead, you'll remain stuck where you are.

hit refresh

Are you making a good salary but find yourself cash poor? Do you find it necessary to make essential purchases on credit cards because you don't have the money in the bank? Do you buy clothes or gadgets for the prestige or bragging rights of having the latest and greatest? Do you feel compelled to keep up with others, even when you can't afford to? If so, like Monica and her husband, you're likely living beyond your means.

Many people are prideful and won't reveal their true financial situation. But by learning to face the reality of your situation, you can find ways to get off of the desire mentality treadmill. Few things create more stress in a relationship than a lack of control in spending. Over-extending yourself based on your pride or momentary impulses can destroy your bank account and your relationships. Break down and ask for help if you need it! You will do yourself, your spouse and your family a favor by admitting that there's a problem. Get the help and begin to live within your means. You'll be surprised at how peaceful you feel!

Each of these links to consumer credit/financial counseling can get you started on a path of change, and lead you to a more solid future. Your bank, credit union and local Chamber of Commerce may also be able to provide names and numbers of professional budgeting and debt counselors. And certainly do an online search of credit and debt counselors in your area to find more resources.

Consumer Credit Counseling
www.consumercredit.com

National Foundation for Credit Counseling
www.nfcc.org/

Money Management International
www.moneymanagement.org

talk to me...

Are you able to keep your financial focus in the face of other people's material displays?

How's your will power holding up?

I want to know.

@CharStallings
facebook.com/iwishbook

chapter 4
do sweat the fine print

Do you remember those credit card offers that bulged out of your mailbox with "0% interest" printed in big bold letters across the envelope? Or how about a $1 life insurance policy? Maybe it was a free cruise vacation getaway to an exotic island?

"That was back in the day Charlotte," you may be thinking. "I remember those offers, but I haven't seen one in a while." I'm glad they're in your memory bank because they were a source of trouble for many people, and we certainly don't want to go back down that path. Easy money offers like those - and consumers' willingness to accept them without critically assessing their cost and value - were a substantial part of the problem that landed our economy in hot water. As far as I'm concerned, we were living in the world of unrestrained "loose lending".

When you opened those offers, they usually said something like - in very fine print of course - *if you're one day late in remitting your payment, the interest rate bumps up to x amount* (or some outrageous amount). Did you take the time to understand, read and ask questions? You may have found yourself paying hundreds, even thousands of dollars more than you expected and you didn't have any legal recourse. Why? Because it was all spelled out for you…in little bitty letters.

I accepted a credit card solicitation a few years ago that offered me a 0% APR for transferring a balance. I was traveling that month and was late on the payment. The next month, my minimum payment had doubled! With one late payment, my interest rate jumped sky high. The bottom line is that I agreed to this. It was on record. I jumped at the offer quickly and didn't spend the time to understand the potential ramifications. ◆

lesson

Always read the fine print on every financial arrangement you are entering into. Before you accept an offer, have a crystal clear understanding of what you are agreeing to. Most importantly, know what actions will be taken if you don't keep up your end of the arrangement so there are no surprises later on.

hit refresh

Read all agreements that have financial implications and don't skip the fine print. This extends to agreements already in place. How often do you receive mail (electronic or hardcopy) regarding changes being made to your existing credit card or bank account agreements? Go ahead and admit it, sometimes we don't think a second about these documents or communications. It's like clockwork – we open the envelope (or email), see all the fine print and say to ourselves, "TMI" (too much information), and then hastily file it away, or toss it in the physical or cyber trash can. I understand that it can feel overwhelming and like a time waster, but reading the fine print is necessary to ensure that you're not in the dark on important financial matters.

Here's a simple way to make sure you stay in the loop on account changes and updates. Starting today, make it a daily or weekly practice to thoroughly read the emails or documents that specifically have to do with changes to your accounts. I call it *power reading* – you take 15 - 30 minutes, minus any distractions, and read your documents. While reading use a pen or pencil to circle or underline any terms or information that are confusing. And by all means, don't hesitate to call the customer service number on the agreement or notification to fully understand what's printed there…..even if it's in 6 pt font.

Here are some agreements whose conditions may change over time or that have clauses you may not have inspected at the start. Check them all carefully.

- Homeowners Association Documents
- Credit cards
- Life Insurance
- Health Insurance (Both Group and Individual Policies)
- Disability Insurance
- Annuities
- IRAs
- Mutual Funds
- Property Tax Assessments

talk to me...

Have you had experience with fine print that rocked your world in a bad way?

What about any 'great catches' before you signed on the dotted line?

Share them with me, I'm interested.

@CharStallings
facebook.com/iwishbook

chapter 5
they show you, believe them

My long time friend, Brian, was known in his neighborhood for working miracles on every kind of machine imaginable, whether it was a lawn mower or a car. He went on to work for a large auto dealership and then, several years later, decided to open his own auto repair shop with a partner. His business partner was an easygoing guy and they got along well, so it never even occurred to Brian that it might be worthwhile to investigate his prospective partner's overall spending habits and money judgments. If he had, he would have discovered a sloppy money manager who didn't budget, save, or even take bills too seriously. Needless to say, the auto repair shop didn't fly and Brian lost a great deal of money.

When you consider doing business with someone, marrying the love of your life, or even moving in with a roommate, look at who they are showing themselves to be in their current financial affairs *and believe it!* This could save you headaches, heartaches and a whole lot of money.

Likewise when my former dorm mate, Terry, first married her husband she noticed that he was very caught up in buying luxury items that he didn't really need, and that the more practical use of money did not concern him. She told me that she saw this behavior early on when they were dating, but she put blinders on and ignored it. She was too excited at the prospect of marrying him to accept the reality that he was probably a poor money manager. She said to me, "Charlotte, **I wish someone had told me** that the way a person spends and handles their money now, is a pretty clear indicator of how they will handle and spend their money in the future. And without help or intervention, those habits are likely not going away." Money issues are one of the top 10 reasons for divorce, and unfortunately, Terry and her husband became a part of that statistic. ◆

lesson

Whether it's a roommate, business partner or spouse, pay attention to how they spend, handle and think about money. If there's a problem now, there is a strong possibility that there will be a greater problem later on.

hit refresh

I'll ask for forgiveness in advance if I've managed to step on your toes because you've run into this situation once or twice before. So the question becomes: are you considering this potential spouse, business partner, or roommate with your eyes wide open about their money practices? Or are you like my friends Brian and Terry, and blinded by the attraction of love, business success, or reduced living expenses?

If you're considering forming a partnership of any kind with someone, here are a few questions you can ask them (and of course any others you may have) to help you better understand their money practices.

1. "What is your debt situation?"
2. "How do you deal with debt?"
3. "What is your practice around talking about money?"
4. "If you received a large, lump sum of money, would you buy a luxury item like a sports car, or pay-down your mortgage?"
5. "Are you open to exchanging copies of credit reports and thoroughly discussing the information in them?"
6. "Would you have any objections to me asking people you've previously been in business with about their experiences in working with you?"

The key is listening to the answers you hear. First, listen with your ears, then set your heart and emotions to the side, and listen (pay attention) with your eyes. By observing their actions and behaviors over a period of time, and in a variety of settings, you can learn a great deal about their money practices. From there you are more equipped to make smart, informed decisions about moving forward with this partnership....or not.

If you're reading this and saying, "Big problem Charlotte, none of this ever crossed my mind before. My new roommate's money habits are totally opposite from mine; I see signs of trouble already. What do I do?" Remember not to panic, rather be thankful for a degree of clarity about the reality of the situation. Consider this an opportunity to build and strengthen your relationship with this individual. Start with a 'sit-down' to share your concerns and observations. No finger pointing or judging, that only hurts; it doesn't help. Instead use this time to understand your financial differences and identify where there are similarities. Gain agreement on guidelines you will implement and adhere to so that obligations are met. The goal is to develop a plan that works for the both of you.

Watch, listen, ask questions and trust your gut!

talk to me...

What sort of money manager is your spouse, business partner, or roommate?

Did you know these things when you walked down the aisle, started your business or got the keys from the landlord?

How have you successfully, or unsuccessfully, dealt with money issues with your spouse, business partner or roommate?

I appreciate your honesty!

@CharStallings
facebook.com/iwishbook

chapter 6

share your goals

If you've decided to buy a franchise or get your Master's Degree or just build a deck on your house, be sure to share your new goal with people around you who are positive and who support you.

When I was in college, I wanted a car really, really bad. I had a close friend who had the same goal. We decided we would have cars of our own by the first day of our senior year. That only gave me the summer months to focus, work hard, and save money. During that summer I was working extra hard as a full-time bank teller, and as a night and weekend dorm counselor at the University of Minnesota. My goal was to save up that whopping $1,000 down-payment by whatever means necessary.

I told my co-workers and family about my goal. This helped for two reasons: First, when I saw them they would ask how I was coming along toward my goal. If I had deposited money in the bank that week, then I couldn't contain my excitement in telling them how I was progressing. But on the other hand, if I had frittered away the money that was earmarked for savings, and not made a bank deposit, then their question irritated me like you couldn't believe. Second, when anyone would ask to borrow money from me I'd quickly tell them, with one hand on my hip and a little bit of a neck roll, "Sorry I can't loan you any money. Every dime I make is going toward my car!"

Here's a word of caution: It's important, no it's absolutely critical, that you share your future financial visions and goals *only* with people who believe in you, who are in agreement with you, and who will encourage you. Watch out for the discouraging pessimists and cynics, they are true naysayers to the core. Some are very forthright in expressing their negativity, and others are more subtle, making biting, little comments or remarks that question the validity of your goals and visions. I call them *goal snatchers*. The sad truth is, they don't have any financial goals, and it infuriates them that you do. Sometimes the biggest pessimists are people who are closest to you. If you find that some people close to you are pessimists, then keep looking for the folks who aren't. Whether the snatchers are subtle or outright, steer clear of them, lest you start second-guessing what you know is right for you.

So what about my car? Classes were starting right after Labor Day, so that Tuesday after work, my brother drove me to the Oldsmobile dealership to start the hunt. We walked every inch of that lot looking for the perfect car. A couple hours later I drove out of there in my new Olds Cierra – it looked like a bumble bee – bright lemon yellow with black interior -- and it was mine! ◆

!lesson

It's a strong motivator when your friends and family understand your goals, and cheer you on in your quest to achieve them.

hit refresh

Start by addressing your WITY – What's Important To You? Get a piece of paper and write down your top three financial goals. Word your goals from a positive perspective and include details. Instead of, "I won't go shopping anymore." Re-word that goal to sound like this, "I will honor my spending plan by allocating money for shopping, and doing so when I can make my purchases in cash." The very act of writing down your goals is an action – it gets the thought out from inside your head and into the light of day. It will be a reminder to you that you need to get it done. Don't second guess yourself about whether your goals are realistic – consider them non-negotiable.

Next, choose one of the goals that you wrote down. Make a plan to tell everyone in your close circle about your goal within one week.

- Do you feel different about that goal?
- Is it more concrete to you?

Start to notice how the goal already seems like a reality now that you've shared it with others.

talk to me...

Did you ever wonder what might have been? Look at those supposedly lost dreams and see if you can salvage one or two of them.

Tell your friends and family about your new goal(s) and see if it doesn't start to take on new life.

Then tell me about it, I want to know too!

@CharStallings
facebook.com/iwishbook

Section II
explore where you want to go - using good judgement, decision-making and strategic skills

need, want or can it wait?

Each time you have the urge to make a purchase, ask yourself this question, "Do I really *need* this, or do I just *want* it?" Only you know if it's within your means or outside of your means, and only you know if you can afford it. Wants can always be deferred and even some needs can be put off. Asking "Can this wait?" is one way to keep talking about money and how you spend it in your household.

This simple strategy does several things. It:
1) Keeps you focused on your financial goals.
2) Creates accountability.
3) Forces you to think.

A few years ago my husband discovered he had purchased more lumber than he needed to repair our fence. I immediately thought we could put the wood to good use by jazzing up our gazebo. (By no means was it a necessary project, but we ran the risk of ruining the wood if it sat outside.)

By this time we had developed a habit of asking ourselves if the purchase we were considering was a need or a want, and what would happen if we waited a specific period of time before making it. (Early in our marriage, we discovered we had confused our wants with our needs. In fact, we jokingly said "We've been deep into the 'wants' category for a long time.")

As we considered the gazebo project, we realized we would need more money than our budget allowed, so we looked at our options. "Can this wait? What will happen if we don't wait?" We ended up putting the lumber in the garage!

Asking these questions helped sustain our commitment to budgeting and achieving our financial goals. ◆

# lesson

It's perfectly fine to say, "It's a need." or you can say, "I know it's a want, and I'm going to develop a plan to be able to pay for it."

# hit refresh

What category are you in these days: want, need or a little of both? Try this simple six step plan to wrap your head around this practice:

1. List all of the things you are considering purchasing for the next 6 – 12 months.
2. Start a conversation with your spouse, a friend or just yourself to put these purchases in perspective.

3. Label each one "want" or "need."

4. Write down the dollar amount each purchase will likely cost.

5. Rank in order the wants and needs.

6. Describe your purchase plan, i.e., pull money from cash reserves, use next quarter's bonus, keep saving, etc.

7. Share your plan with someone close to you and ask them to check on your progress from time to time. Promise to take them out to dinner when you achieve your goals.

Example:

Purchases	Want/Need	$ Amount	Rank Order	Purchase Plan
BMW 5 Series	Want	27,000	3	3
Personal Trainer 3x/ week	Need & Want	2,500	2	2
Summer Camp (for daughter)	Need	1,150	1	1

This exercise will help you get clarity on your plans for managing the needs and wants in your life. Consider how much money you can save or invest if you only satisfied some of your needs in the short term.

Another suggestion is to apply the simple "Can It Wait" test. Here are some guidelines that have worked well for me:

1. Wait at least one week before making a major purchase.

2. Always ask, "Can I wait?" "What are other options?" "What will happen if I don't wait?"

3. Use the "If, then" question. "If I make this purchase or spend this money, then _____ will happen."

talk to me...

Have you ever confused your wants with your needs, and experienced a disastrous outcome?

How do you work out your spending priorities today?

I'd love to hear about it!

@CharStallings
facebook.com/iwishbook

chapter 8

credit discipline

Do you have lots of credit cards and find yourself making minimum payments each month? Or maybe you only have one or two cards, but those cards are the backbone of your budget? If you couldn't charge everything on them, you would have a hard time making it. If charging is a big part of your life, tell me, when do you think you will be out of debt? Did you know that the interest you are paying on those cards far exceeds the actual amount that you owe? What is the vicious cycle of charging and paying the minimum doing to you financially? Credit card companies don't expect you to be disciplined. That's how they make their money. Devise a plan to control your spending, and your debt, and take back your money and your life.

Credit can be a very effective tool, but it must be managed wisely and with discipline. At one time, I had lots of credit cards and I was paying the minimum on all of them! I thought I was impressing the sales associates at the checkout counter when I would flip through several Visas and MasterCards, and ultimately settle on the store card like Macy's, Nordstrom's, or Saks that I wanted to use for that purchase. Quite honestly, I wasn't impressing anyone, but rather publicly showing how poor of a money manager I was. You see, while I was whipping through those cards, in my mind I was trying to quickly figure out which one(s) I had paid, and on which ones I could charge. It really was a sick little game I learned to play!

Here's how it started and how it went each month: first card offer comes in the mail, sign up without reading details, card arrives - go straight to mall, instantly charge up the full balance on that card, bill arrives, send minimum payment. Next card offer arrives, sign up.......you see the pattern? Credit cards are not bad or evil, it's the lack of discipline around using them that created problems for me and so many others.

Credit card companies don't expect you to be disciplined.

I finally realized that it would take me a long time to pay off my debt if I just paid the minimum on each card. Another bad habit I had was to go out and charge more once I had made a payment. Imagine the enormous amount of interest I would have paid if I had continued that practice! When I finally looked at the fact that I charged *everything* from gasoline to clothes to groceries (immediate consumables), and I was paying outrageous interest on these purchases, that's when I realized my charging habits were out of control.◆

lesson

Have a structured approach to using credit cards, and stick with it!

hit refresh

If you want things to change altogether, you must do things altogether differently. Here's a simple plan to help curb your charging habits:

1. Stop the madness! Put the credit cards on lock-down. I mean give them a full-on, much-needed rest by asking a friend or family member to hold on to them. If it's too easy to finagle and get the cards back, then cut them up! Yep, snip snip is precisely what I mean. You know what, you can even 'put them on ice' – literally. Trust me, credit cards entombed in a bowl of water in the freezer can put a dent in the best made shopping plans. If you're rolling your eyes and thinking, "this woman is crazy! Put my credit cards in the freezer....I don't think so!" Well I'll just say this, sometimes extreme measures are necessary to address extreme situations. I'm sharing with you some steps I've taken at different times in my life to gain control over my then out-of-control charging habits. What's important is that you understand your habits, and decide if those habits are good or not. If not, figure out approaches that will work for you, to help you get things under control.

2. No shortcuts. Have you ever committed your credit card numbers to memory, or you have them listed in a special encrypted app on your iPhone or Droid? Maybe you depend on the sales clerk or customer service rep to easily retrieve your card information at checkout with a valid I.D. These shortcuts and tricks are games we play that ambush our plans to use more discipline in our charging and spending. Do you really win and move forward when you use these tactics? Not at all. Like many areas in life, to make changes in our charging habits, it starts with making a choice – our mindset must change. Work hard to resist the urges to splurge. Nancy Reagan said it best years ago, "Just say no!"

3. Cash and carry. Set aside an amount of money in an envelope each week (or pay period) after you've met all obligations on your budget. This money is specifically for the purchases you would have put on your credit card. If you see an item you want to buy, instead of swiping your card, whip out your envelope and pull out some cold, hard cash to pay for the item. You can now really enjoy the item because there's no bill to pay later on, what a great feeling!

4. Wait for it. If you find something you want and you don't have enough cash at the time, wait until the next week, or the week after, or for goodness sake the next month to buy it. You're practicing discipline, and at the same time really deciding if it's worth saving extra money each week to be able to get it.

talk to me...

Have you played the credit card game?

What made you decide to stop? How do you use credit cards now?

Care to share? I'd like to know!

@CharStallings
facebook.com/iwishbook

chapter 9
the brand new car

Have you ever dreamed of driving home a brand new car...what a feeling, right? Wrong! How about buying that dream outfit at The Galleria for the big event next month, an outfit you will probably wear once, maybe twice at best, and then store it away forever?

These are examples of momentary sensations that give us a thrill. What about the long-term feeling of losing tens of thousands of dollars on a vehicle that starts depreciating the minute you drive it off of the lot? And how do you feel about that barely-worn outfit hanging in the back of the closet?

A few years ago, my husband decided that a brand new Nissan Altima was just what we needed to get around town. It had a new body style, handled great on the road, and most importantly it was very fuel efficient. While it was a huge treat and surprise to see this shiny new car in the driveway, it wasn't the best move because we hadn't really budgeted for it. After talking and analyzing the numbers, we decided to trade the car in on a different, pre-owned vehicle. It was shocking to find out what the dealership would offer us for a *virtually unused* car. We could not get anything close to the retail price. Since then, we decided that pre-owned is all we're interested in, if the car isn't at least three years old, we don't want it. ◆

lesson

Buying brand new, especially a car, really only satisfies your ego.

hit refresh

These days there are more opportunities than ever to save money by purchasing high-quality, pre-owned goods. Of course online options abound so do an exhaustive internet search to see what you can find. Here are a few other ideas:

- Check out designer labels at your local consignment stores, a favorite in my neighborhood is www.karenscloset.com.
- Need a special western outfit for the rodeo? Check out www.ebay.com or www.craigslist.com. I have a cowgirl wannabe friend who sells off her new rodeo clothes on these websites every year after the Houston rodeo shuts down.
- I have another friend who regularly buys and sells her fast-growing kids' clothes and bedroom furniture on www.ebay.com, she swears by it.
- For great formalwear without the great big price tag, check out www. renttherunway.com (they ship to you) or www.onenightaffair.com (if you're in the Los Angeles area).
- As an admitted cool handbag addict, here's my personal favorite: www. bagborroworsteal.com where you can rent designer handbags, jewelry, sunglasses and watches. (I loved the Gucci Large Babouska Tote that

retails at $1,195 and rents out for $75 a month.) On this site you can also buy pre-owned authentic designer bags and accessories for a fraction of the cost. Just think, you can get all the sizzle and sensation, for just cents on the dollar. My kind of shopping indeed!

And if you're shopping for a car, first decide that pre-owned is a good option, it's perfectly fine to let someone else take that new car hit. Then check out the average retail price on Kelly Blue Book at www.kbb.com to give you greater negotiating power when looking for the kind of car you want. Look for safety and performance in cars three-years-old or older. If you don't see what you're looking for right now, stay in contact with the pre-owned car sales manager at your favorite dealership. They can tell you when those two- or three-year executive leases are up on the car you're interested in. Generally these cars have been well-maintained... and they even still smell new.

When you do find what you want, and you've inked the deal, look at the asking prices for brand new cars of the same model. That's a lot of money you've saved. Pat yourself on the back and if you can, put the amount you've saved (or some of it) in the bank as a "thank you" to yourself.

# talk to me...

Where do you go to find good deals on things you need and want?

Hey, I'd love to add it to my list!

@CharStallings
facebook.com/iwishbook

chapter 10

budget isn't a cussword

Would you casually say to a friend during a quick conversation, or to your spouse over breakfast, "Let's take a two week vacation, starting today!" Imagine, simply walking out the door and driving to the airport. Deciding as you enter the terminal where to go and then purchasing your tickets for the next flight. You would have no luggage, no time off from work and no idea what you would do when you arrived at your destination. While this could be the adventure of a lifetime, frankly, this approach to travel sounds a little crazy, doesn't it? Yet, this is how some people handle their monthly and yearly spending.

I wish someone had told me that creating a spending plan (better known as a budget), for all of my expenses, as well as my short- and long-term goals and purchases, could be empowering and liberating. Knowing that I can achieve my goals, and that I have a method of staying on track with spending, saving and investing gives me peace of mind.

In the early days of marriage, my husband and I paid our bills but we weren't putting any money aside for later. Keeping to our "don't ask, don't tell" style, we kept our money separate and didn't really talk about it. When we finally began creating a budget together that reflected our joint income, all expenses, saving and purchase goals, we began to talk about our shared dreams and ideas. I realized then just how much we had needed a planned approach to our spending. Having a budget doesn't mean you *can't* make purchases, rather it is a way to plan to get the things that you want. Until this time, I was hostile toward the idea of a budget. I felt restricted by it.

It was quite a revelation when I learned that a budget is a tool that offers so many benefits. A budget, I found:

1. Helps me see what comes in and what goes out.
2. Creates a framework or structure for managing my finances.
3. Fosters personal accountability.
4. Supports and develops clear communication.
5. Uncovers opportunities to save or reduce spending.
6. Keeps me righteous!

Item #6 on the list above is a big one. Having a budget in place, that I honored and abided by, has kept me from giving in to temptations, which allowed me to accomplish the financial goals I had established. I remember several years ago when I wanted to surprise my husband with an incredible (and expensive) anniversary gift, I knew the only way I could pull this off was to stay on course with my budget. There was no room for deviation at all, not one cent. So that meant, for a period of time, DSW drive-by's (even with a coupon) were out. Charming Charlie's (one of my favorite jewelry and accessory stores on the planet) swing-thru's were history. It also meant foregoing a few hair and nail appointments to make this work (if I was stretching out the hair and nail visits, you *know* I was serious about this surprise).

Was I tempted? Every single day I was tempted! But I forced myself to remember how bad I felt when I veered off course in the past and I wasn't able to do what I had planned. I also remembered how satisfied and happy I felt when I had stayed on track with my budget, and achieved certain goals I had set. I preferred the good feeling over the bad one, and with that quick stroll down memory lane, I brushed the temptation aside and remained focused on the end result.

Speaking of end results, seeing my husband's face when he saw his anniversary gift that year was priceless! I cannot tell you how great it felt to know that I had developed a plan (and stuck to it) to guide my spending that would allow me to do something pretty cool for him. By now you're probably asking, "So what was the gift Charlotte?" It was ……. ….nah, I'll let it remain our little secret! ◆

lesson

A budget is simply a roadmap to get from one point to another with your finances.

hit refresh

The best way to create a budget is to start talking. (Yes, I've said it again. Talk about money!) Make an appointment with your spending partner(s) to talk about and write down:

A. What your household income is each month.
B. What your fixed, variable and periodic expenses are.

C. What all your outstanding debts amount to (balances, minimum payments, interest rates etc.).

D. Who do you owe? When do you owe it? How much do you owe them?

Also discuss future purchases (for the home, cars, education, trips, etc.) and how you can accomplish these goals.

Create a master list of income and expenses and begin to manage your money, each time you're paid, to this list. You can use a yellow pad, an Excel spreadsheet, or free online tools at sites like www.budgetsimple.com or www.budgettracker. com. Alternatively, you can use apps on your tablet or smartphone like Mint, Pageonce or Easy Money - just make sure you're operating on a budget.

talk to me...

Is your budget kept strictly in your memory? Or is it jotted down on the back of your utility bill envelope?

What does your budget look like? How has it evolved over time?

Give me the real story.

@CharStallings
facebook.com/iwishbook

the envelope, please!

Okay, I'll admit it, sometimes being accountable and sticking to a budget is not so easy. When the money's in the bank and you're writing a check, using a debit or credit card, it's easy to forget that you're spending concrete dollars and cents. Try carrying around an envelope for the week with your grocery money or your gas money in it. I bet you'll learn a few things about sticking to your budget then!

This strategy is very old, and I'm grateful we were introduced to it. When my husband and I decided to attack our debt, pay down our bills and pay off the credit cards, we got some envelopes. Here's what you do. Take the amount for groceries for example, say $300 a month, and put it in an envelope. My friend Ros laughed out loud when I shared this example with her. "Try $300 a week Charlotte!" she chuckled. (The key is to use numbers that are realistic for *your* family. And where do we find these numbers? On our budget, of course!)

As you spend the money, write an account of your spending on the front of the envelope. It might sound cumbersome but envelopes work like a charm to keep you on track with your budget, and help you actually pay off bills – both big and small. I'll always remember this woman at our church who begrudgingly shared with me one day that she and her husband used envelopes. She didn't particularly like carrying envelopes around, in fact she used to whine about it to her husband (and anyone who would listen) quite often. But as quickly as she voiced her displeasure, she would say, "I'll be the first to admit I hate The Envelope System, but the reality is, using it allowed us to pay off our house way before the 30-year timeframe. We haven't had a mortgage payment in a long, long time." Mind you, this wasn't a retired couple in their 60's or 70's, they were just a few years older than us

By using envelopes you may realize that you didn't need as much money for a particular line item, or you may determine that you needed more. The envelope method allows you to track actual spending and see what puts you over and under budget. To this day, it's the only thing that my husband and I can fall back on to keep us on course. For this to work, everybody has to be committed. There has to be accountability. If I run out of my spending money and I rob the gas money; that doesn't work. ◆

lesson

Using envelopes can be a simple, solid way to manage money more efficiently.

hit refresh

1. Start with picking one line item from your budget, like groceries or gas, something that can tend to fluctuate.

2. Withdraw that amount of cash from your bank account and put it in an envelope. Label the envelope with the budget item and amount.

3. Take the envelope with you when it's time to shop or fill-up.

4. At check-out time, pay for your purchase(s) with the cash in the envelope. If you don't have enough money, take things out of your grocery cart and give them to the cashier. Just say, "I changed my mind on this item." Those in line behind you will be just fine.

5. Record your remaining cash (new balance) on the envelope.

6. After several weeks, assess if you've budgeted too much or not enough for that particular line item. I guarantee that you will see some type of pattern emerge over time.

talk to me...

What do you think about using envelopes? It sounds simple, do you think you can do it?

Have you ever put something back because you didn't have the money to pay for it?

Drop me a line and tell me your thoughts.

@CharStallings
facebook.com/iwishbook

chapter 12
don't bank on your bonus

From 2008 to now, you can hardly blink without hearing about layoffs, workforce reductions, plant closures and more. In fact, as I proofed this manuscript, the iconic Hostess Brands was on the brink of closing their doors forever. Despite tough economic conditions in recent years, our economy is slowly improving and various industries and sectors are experiencing growth. With growth comes bonuses – halleleujah, bring on the bonuses! Some people will receive monthly, quarterly or annual bonuses according to their individual productivity, or their payout may be based on the overall performance of their organization. If you are expecting a bonus in the near future, I challenge you to think of that money, not as a part of your salary, but as an unpredictable extra, even if you're saying, "But, I've been receiving this extra money for over three years!"

To that, I would say, "Things change. Be prepared."

If your lifestyle can't be supported without your bonus money, I suggest that you look at streamlining and simplifying. Your lifestyle, most likely has more flexibility to it than you realize.

Regardless of the industry or sector, jobs in sales can be some of the most lucrative because of the hefty bonuses and commissions paid. I've been fortunate to have worked in several sales positions, one of which was directly tied to the investment markets. When the markets were up and performing well, bonuses were great. But when the markets were down, I was unhappy at bonus time. After several years of steadily increasing quarterly bonuses, I started making big purchases in anticipation of my next bonus check. It only took one major market correction to teach me a hard lesson. My next bonus check was a fraction of what I'd been getting. I was miserable! I had factored a dollar amount into our budget and modified our lifestyle to reflect it. This was a bad move! ◆

lesson

A bonus is a windfall - a piece of unexpected financial, good fortune. Treat it like it was exactly that….unexpected.

hit refresh

1. Wean yourself off of your bonuses. Don't factor this extra money into your regular living expense budget. In fact, call it a windfall or gravy, and think of it as such.
2. Save your bonus and spend it for planned purchases only.
3. Allocate your bonuses specifically toward long-term goals like education,

retirement or other dreams you have.

4. Consider using the "Rule of Thirds" with your bonus money, as a reward of sorts for achieving certain goals. It's simple:
   - Pay yourself 1/3.
   - Save or invest 1/3.
   - Use the remaining 1/3 for purchases.

Do you get a bonus on your job? Is it only at certain times of the year?

How do you spend, save or invest it?

I'm curious to hear your take on dealing with bonuses.

@CharStallings
facebook.com/iwishbook

chapter 13
shopping when you're sad

Emotional purchases cannot make you happy. Take it from me, when the going gets tough, don't go shopping. Let me say that another way: Buying stuff when you are feeling needy or exuberant, does nothing except make someone else richer. When you are hungry, eat something from the fridge or your pantry. When you go grocery shopping hungry or upset, you may find yourself back in the your kitchen unloading Baked Lays potato chips, gummy bears, Blue Bell ice-cream, chocolate chip cookies, Moon Pies and HEB Rotisserie Chicken Salad wondering, "What was I thinking?"

The same idea applies to shopping for clothes or other products. Did you have a fight with the one you love? Now is not the best time to visit your favorite electronic media store. Feeling angry at your boss? That shoe store on the way home is not the best place to go for comfort. Instead, when you've got the blues, pick up the phone and call a friend. Go for a long walk and if you must buy something, buy a cup of coffee or a magazine for yourself. Why not give yourself the gift of an iTunes download, or an actual CD, and let the music mellow you.

After college, I landed a great job, and I got my first American Express card. This charge card gave me a feeling of achievement with real purchasing power, which I took advantage of and enjoyed because I had been a broke college student for so long. On my job, sometimes I would be overwhelmed or stressed out, and whenever I felt this way, I would go shopping. I spent many a Saturday, and most of my money, buying things to make me feel better. I was enjoying it and making the tough stuff go away (or so I thought). For me, shopping was a mask to cover up whatever I was depressed or frustrated about. In the end, I didn't feel any better and I would often take the clothes back.

I didn't know it then, but I suffered from *emotional spending*. An article I read recently on this topic suggested that everyone should consider their emotional state when shopping. "People tend to over-shop when they are in extreme emotional states: too happy or too sad. Very happy people like to believe there is a need for a celebration which could be an excuse for over-spending, while people who are emotionally down find solace in shopping for things to comfort themselves. They want to believe that shopping fills the emptiness they are feeling." So if you are in either of these emotional states, staying at home, instead of going to the mall, is by far a better option.

There are hundreds of ways to deal with stress and anxiety that do not involve a credit card or a check book.

To be honest, sometimes the *emotional spending* bad habit rears its ugly head back up, and if I'm not careful, I've snapped into counterproductive habits in a heartbeat. **I wish someone had told me** that there are hundreds of ways to deal with stress and anxiety that do not involve a credit card or a check book. When I only buy what I need most of the time, I can afford to buy what I *really want* later. That's a nice feeling!

These days, when I'm feeling edgy, I call up my mother or sister and laugh. Sometimes I play catch with our little Yorkie and his gnawed up toys, or I just sit and giggle with my daughter or talk to my husband about nothing in particular. Whatever I do these days to deal with the blues, I know it doesn't involve spending money! ◆

lesson

Spending when you're hurting or happy isn't helpful, it just makes matters worse.

hit refresh

I agree with the folks at www.Investopia.com who say, "While avoiding emotional spending completely is probably not a realistic goal for most people, learning to recognize and curb your emotional spending can be an important tool." We all make emotional purchases from time to time. When you have a habit of boosting your excitement, or numbing your pain by making purchases, then you have a habit that's hurting you. Find things to substitute for shopping when you're abounding or blue.

Here are a few recommendations from Investopia to decrease the damage emotional spending does to your wallet.

1. **Avoid making impulse buys** – whether in a physical store or online. Train yourself to wait before making any buying decisions. (See chapter on Needs vs. Wants.)

2. **Limit your exposure to advertising** – unsubscribe, opt-out and block ads that show up in your inbox. If need be, switch to public radio in the car, and cancel magazine subscriptions so you're not tempted by the beautiful, glossy ads.

3. **Limit your exposure to tempting situations** – reduce your mall visits or time dedicated to online shopping.

4. **Find ways to hold yourself accountable for your spending** – look to the people you live with or spend the most time with to help you.

5. **Find more constructive behaviors to help you deal with emotional spending.** This step has been the most important for me; here are some ideas I turn to:

   - Walk the dog around the neighborhood
   - Ride my bike to the park
   - Get lost in 30 minutes of reality T.V.
   - Phone a friend or family member
   - Put on my Beats by Dre and sing to the top of my lungs
   - Put on my Beats by Dre and dance like crazy
   - Play Spider Solitare or Spades online
   - Check out Facebook
   - Read a magazine article
   - Take a nap

These things work for me. Now develop your own list of ideas that will lift *your* mood, and make sure you have it handy when you experience a need-to-shop attack.

talk to me...

What do you do to work off stress?

Have you changed your impulsive buying habits? How did you do it?

Write and tell me. I'm interested.

@CharStallings
facebook.com/iwishbook

chapter 14
it's okay to say no

Loaning money to family and friends is a way to help them get by when they are in a tight spot. When someone approaches you for a loan, be clear in your own mind and with them concerning the guidelines for the loan. And make sure it's an amount of money that you can afford to give away.

You are accountable for *your* financial health, not someone else's. Be calm, clear and friendly, but make your boundaries understood. "This is what I can afford to loan you."

If this is an ongoing loan arrangement, make sure it works for you over time. What worked last month may not work this month. Look long and hard at habitually giving money to someone who is unable to pay you back and wants more money more often.

Historically in my family I played the role of caretaker, buying gifts, helping around the house and springing for extra cash if someone needed help. At one point, one of my brothers needed help paying for his daughter's daycare. Two weeks later, he came to me again…and then again in another two weeks. A pattern was developing.

Soon I started to fall behind on my bills. I was concerned and I saw no end to the regular money requests. I asked the pastor at my church what to do. He said, "Follow the $25 rule. Decide how much you can afford to give away each month that will not hurt you. Maybe it's $25 or $250. Whatever the amount, say to yourself, "If I never get this back, I'll be okay."

Sure enough I received another request. I agreed to help and told him to come to my office to get it. He came in and I handed him an envelope. He thanked me, took the envelope and walked out. At the elevator I heard him exclaim, "What?" He rushed back into my office. "This is just $25!"

"Yep," I said, "It's $25 – you can take it or leave it. He left it and that was the end of those requests. Up until that day, I had felt powerless around how I could be supportive but not put myself in jeopardy. Now, I have a plan to support those I care about, including me.

It's also possible that you just can't afford to give *any* money away. In that case, say so!

Saying no to a family member was stressful for me but now I understand that knowing how to say *no* says a lot about your judgment, peace of mind and financial stability. **I wish someone had told me**, "When you are swayed by the winds of other people's fortunes and requests, you can end up being blown over." Stand your ground and understand that you cannot fix every situation, and you cannot *please* everyone. ◆

 lesson

You are the only person taking care of your money, if you let misplaced guilt or a *rescue instinct* influence you, you could end up without the money that you really need.

 hit refresh

Take a long, hard look at your finances:

- Can you afford to give any money away? Yes or No (circle one)
- How much? $_____
- If you have a habit of loaning people money that you can't afford to give away, ask yourself, "What is the pay-off for me to continue this activity?"

_____

_____

- Does it make you feel needed? Yes or No (circle one)
- Can you find other ways to contribute that are not monetary? Yes or No (circle one) List these: _____

_____

If you have a specific amount of money each month that you have committed to saving, try to honor that commitment. You need *you* more than they need you, so make your boundaries clear and stick with them, for your sake and theirs.

Setting a specific limit on how much you are willing to loan is exactly about doing what works for you. When you do what works for you financially, you empower yourself toward successful management in all areas of your life.

And here is a suggestion on what you can do when the only appropriate answer is *no*. Confide in a friend about your situation and ask for their help in a role playing exercise. Ask them to play the role of the person who has asked you for money and have a practice conversation in front of a mirror, saying, "I've thought about your request and I've decided not to give you any money."

talk to me...

Have you ever struggled to tell a friend or relative that you could not loan or give them money?

How did that conversation work out?

What do you do today?

Thanks for sharing!

@CharStallings
facebook.com/iwishbook

chapter 15
bill collectors – deal with them

It is my belief that we all sometimes like to simply become invisible and hope that unpleasant things will pass. Some of those unpleasant things can include juggling past-due bills and managing the bill collectors who hunt us down to get those payments. The truth is there are only two ways to successfully deal with bill collectors: 1) pay them or 2) talk to them and work out a payment plan.

Not long after finishing college, I got a great job as a cash management officer in a large bank. I loved it and when that job ended, I became very depressed, even though I got another good job at Xerox. I was working, had a good income and living at home with my mother at the time. So my expenses were low, but my spending was out of control and I wasn't handling my bills correctly, they were delinquent and piling up. Bill collectors started to call me and I just ignored them.

As a banker, my mother understood the ramifications of not dealing with the collectors. She was sick and tired of seeing notices arrive in the mail, and watching me avoid certain phone calls. So, we had a 'come to Jesus meeting'. She forced me to sit down and talk....no, it was more like sit down and listen! She said, "Charlotte, this is ridiculous; you can't continue this way. You are making a mess of your finances. You must change your spending habits, and you must pay your bills. Figure out how much money you can send to each creditor, and then *call them* to let them know how you intend to get things back in order. If you continue avoiding them, they're going to keep sending collection notices and calling you here at home, and then they'll start calling you on your new job."

I just had to face it, and more importantly, handle it!

Well we couldn't have that could we? I had no desire to have bill collectors calling me at Xerox - not cool at all! As much as I didn't want to hear any of this, and as embarrassed as I was for letting things get so out of control, I knew my mother was right. And here's the crazy part: I knew exactly all the steps and actions collectors would take because I used to be a student loan and mortgage loan collector when I was in college. Silly me! Maybe I thought I had special immunity or something. Anyway, I took my mother's advice. Nervous and ashamed, I sat down with a pen and paper, and I called every single creditor and said, "Here's what I can pay now and do over time to get current, will you accept this?" To my surprise, they all said yes, of course. After making all those calls, and having those conversations, I felt such a relief, a huge burden, that I had created, was now lifted. To tell the truth, those calls weren't nearly as bad as I thought they would be. What could have blown up in my face became a manageable situation. I'm glad my mother told me that I just had to face it, and more importantly, handle it!

Did you know that a calm, firm manner and a knowledge of your rights as a debtor is a loud signal to a collector that you are someone with whom they can negotiate?

Under the law, a bill collector can do the following things in response to your failure to pay:

- They can call you at home each day within certain hours.
- They can report your late payment to credit bureaus.
- They can cancel your service or repossess the item(s) that you bought from them.
- They can place a lien on a piece of your property.

You, on the other hand, can ask for such things as no or lower interest and a payment plan or, in some extreme cases, to pay only a percentage of what you owe. It's important to understand your rights and then pick up the phone and call your creditors. Here are a few things to know.

The Fair Debt Collection Practices Act (FDCP) applies to any personal, family or household debt and covers debt collectors who regularly collect debts for others. The FDCP does not apply to the original creditors or their attorneys. As a consumer, you have certain rights under the provisions of the FDCP Act.

- Debt collectors are prohibited from harassing, oppressing or abusing you.
- They cannot threaten to take your property without having the legal right to do so.
- They cannot use false statements that imply they are attorneys or indicate they work for a credit bureau, the Social Security Administration, or another authoritative agency.

The law further prohibits debt collectors from:

- Contacting you at inconvenient times (defined as before 8:00 AM or after 9:00 PM) or places.

- The collector may not contact you at work if your employer disapproves, but you must notify the debt collector of this in writing via certified mail.
- They are forbidden to tell anyone else that you are behind on your debts.
- They cannot use obscene or abusive language. ◆

lesson

It is important to be proactive in managing your debt or your credit could suffer lasting damage. Do your best to contact your creditors right away and work out a payment plan that you both find acceptable.

hit refresh

Before you pick up the phone to call your creditors, know what you can and cannot do to pay down or settle the debt. This is not the time to be pushed into a commitment that you are unable to keep. Be polite and honest. Say, "I am not unwilling to pay, I am simply *unable to pay at this time.*" If you can't come to an agreement at that time, thank them for talking with you and ask them if you can think about the conversation and call them back another time. Don't wait too long to call back because the longer you wait, the worse things may get with that creditor, and your credit report.

Here are some steps to follow when you are faced with debt.

1. Research the lowest interest rates on your credit cards and at your bank and find out if you can consolidate all of your debts into one low interest rate debt. You may need to negotiate a lower interest rate with one of your credit card companies.

2. Call your creditor and tell them what you can feasibly afford to pay and in what timeframe. See if you can reach a payment plan agreement with them.

3. Look at your finances carefully and see if you have any extra money that you can use to apply toward this debt. It may be an extra $30 - $50 a month that you can save by cutting back on cable channels, or premium movie service. Once you have found some extra money, begin applying it to your debt payment.

4. When you have paid off one debt, take the money you were using for that debt and begin applying it to the next debt. Snowball it!

5. Do your best not to create new debt!

talk to me...

Have you ever calmly negotiated with bill collectors? How did that work out for you?

Have you avoided bill collectors? What happened?

Tell me how you handled it, I'm interested?

@CharStallings
facebook.com/iwishbook

Section III
execute your plans - commit to go forward

save or pay off debt?

Whenever I speak to a group about money management, I am always asked this question, "Should I save my money or pay off the bills?" My reply, "Work hard to pay off your debt before you earnestly try to save."

From an emotional standpoint it can be gratifying to know that you are putting money aside *and* paying your bills as well. But while saving money may feel great you are, in reality, rewarding yourself with far more money if you pay off your debt as quickly as possible. Why? Because credit card and installment loan interest rates are typically higher than the interest you would earn on a money market account or Certificate of Deposit. This is a no-brainer, get the debt paid down quickly!

I remember feeling frustrated when all of my hard-earned income was going towards paying bills. I had a pity-party every single payday. And when I considered the fact that I alone had built this mountain of debt, I became even more irritated. "I should have a big, fat savings account by now!" is what I mumbled to myself as I wrote the checks to send to my creditors, and I was right. **I wish someone had told me** back then that it's easy to save and invest when you have disposable income, and to create disposal income, I needed to pay off my debt as fast as I could. ◆

lesson

One key to financial freedom is paying off debt so you are free to save, invest and build wealth on a regular basis.

hit refresh

The *snowball approach* is the most effective way I know of to pay off bills. It's not a quick-fix gimmicky process, but rather a disciplined practice that can work wonders for you, even if you are in serious debt. Trust me, I know firsthand that it works, snowballing and envelopes helped me and my husband get our financial lives in order.

Here's how it works.

First, look around (literally and figuratively) to *find extra money* that can be applied to your debt each month. Why? Because if you only pay the minimums on all of your debts you will pay some insane amount, which will be significantly more than you originally spent or charged. This extra money may come from canceling the gym membership that you never use, or cutting back on daily Venti Caramel Macchiatos to twice a week, or limiting shoe purchases (there I go again) to two pair instead of four. The goal is to find at least $25 (more is better) that you can commit to paying toward your debt, every month, for as long as it takes to clear it all out.

Next, organize your bills in a table format (see example below), from the lowest outstanding balance to the highest outstanding balance. Include your minimum monthly payment amounts, and interest rates if you like (but not necessary). You can put this information in a spreadsheet or write it on a notepad. The key is having it written down. It will be easier to follow and monitor, and it's rewarding and motivating to track your progress.

Bill & Outstanding Balance	Min Pymt	Extra Found Money	Pd Mo #1	Pd Mo #2	Pd Mo #3	Pd Mo #4	Pd Mo #5	Pd Mo #6	Pd Mo #7	Pd Mo #8	Pd Mo #9	Pd Mo #10	Pd Mo #11	Pd Mo #12
Visa – $300	$50	$50	100	100	100	---	---	----	---	---	---	---	---	-----
Macy's - $600	$60	----	60	60	60	160	160	100	---	---	---	---	---	-----
Cred. Union - $1,600	$110	----	110	110	110	110	110	170	270	270	270	70	---	-----
Car Pymt - $4,000	$275	----	275	275	275	275	275	275	275	275	275	475	545	505

Then, take your *extra found money* and add it to the minimum payment for your first bill that has the lowest outstanding balance. Pay this amount each month until that bill is paid in full.

Then, when the first bill is paid off, take the total amount you were contributing to it and add it to the minimum payment for the second bill. The idea is that with each bill or account, the amount you're paying grows larger -- like a snowball rolling down a hill. As the snowball rolls down the hill it picks up steam and rolls faster and faster. The same idea applies to your bills – you're paying them off quicker and quicker. For example, in the above chart the Visa would have been paid off in six months with minimum monthly payments. Snowballing knocked it out in three months! And likewise with Macy's and the credit union, what should've been 10- and 15-month payoffs, were accomplished in half that time. It really does work!

Continue this process until you are making extra payments on your biggest bill, like your mortgage. And above all, don't create any new debt unless it's absolutely necessary.

Sidebar: An exception to paying your bills before saving money is your employer-sponsored retirement plan. I suggest you contribute the maximum amount that you can each pay period. It helps to reduce your taxable income and you get the company match. This is systematic investing at its best!

talk to me...

Do you encounter challenges when focusing on paying off debt?

How do you feel when you finally pay a bill in full?

I want to hear from you.

@CharStallings
facebook.com/iwishbook

chapter 17
do the hustle

No, I am not jamming to Night Fever by the Bee Gees, and you should not dig out your favorite disco track either! This chapter is as far from white, flare-leg, 3-piece pant suits, gold lame` halter dresses, and chunky platform shoes as I can think of. It is, instead, about asking yourself what extra things you can do to generate income for you and your family. Think about it, if you have just one way to make money and for some reason or another that goes south, what can you do to maintain your cash flow? How about some type of side gig, or additional work tied to something you love, that brings in extra money? Do *you* have a hustle?

The best way to develop this side gig is to look at all of your skills, talents, gifts and abilities. You may know right off the bat what those are, or you may have to figure it out. Do you have a hobby or a secret passion? Look at turning it into a money-making activity. Are you a gifted seamstress, mechanic or coach? There is hidden money in your talents, why not put them to use and watch the extra dollars add up each month?

Most everyone, I believe, has a talent or gift that can generate money. I have a friend who works full-time for a major airline; she has also kept her cosmetology license active for the past 20 years. She does hair on the weekends to make extra money, but most importantly it provides security in an industry (and an economy) that is subject to layoffs. My mother has transformed her crocheting hobby into a special order retail business, and many of her items are sold at specialty boutiques. What about you? What skills, gifts, talents and abilities do you have that can be transformed into a money-making enterprise?

Here are a few examples of how friends and family have created side gigs, and turned their talents into income streams:

- A cousin cuts hair after work.
- A friend does auto detailing on the weekends.
- A friend provides pick-up & drop-off shoe shining services.
- Another friend does faux painting after finishing her early morning shift.
- A family member consults and strategizes with businesses across the world.

I know that all talents don't materialize overnight. Many are born out of sheer determination and hard work, and subsequently develop over time. My husband started collecting art a couple years before we got married. While he was developing a passion for beautiful prints, the cost of custom picture-framing was exorbitant. After our wedding, we took a framing course at the local university. Soon, we had framed every piece we owned. Those early pieces weren't so great, in fact they were pretty pitiful (we still have our first once) but the more we framed, the better we got. We both had full-time jobs, but after dinner most days of the week, we would go to our basement to cut glass and mat boards. We would then assemble the piece, and join the corners of the wood

What skills, gifts, talents and abilities do you have that can be transformed into a money-making enterprise?

and metal frames. All ready for pick-up by our customers. Not long after getting started, friends and family were asking us to frame their art. Before we knew it, we were framing pictures every evening and all-day on weekends in our basement…and we were making good money! What started as a hobby - picture-framing – blossomed into a full-fledged hustle.

Now if you're slipping into a, "I don't have a skill or hobby" sing-a-long in your mind, stop it right now! There is another way to approach this: look for a problem that you or others you know, have encountered and set out to fix it. Consider this, if you can provide a solution to a legitimate need, people will buy!

Here's a perfect example. The decorative concrete detailing on our driveway was beginning to dull after a few years. We tried to get our builder to restore the finish to its original luster and condition, but he wasn't interested, plus the builder's warranty had long expired, so no luck there. We tried to get the company that originally poured the driveway concrete to fix it, but the job was too small for them, so they were not an option. We desperately researched and called other concrete businesses in our area, but to no avail, nobody was interested in this work. Were we ticked off? We sure were! After months and months of searching, we realized the business provider we needed did not exist. After complaining about it for a few weeks, we finally had an "aha moment". Maybe this was an opportunity for us to be our own service provider, and to build a side gig at the same time. Voila, a new business was born! ◆

lesson

That little thing you do on the side can generate important, sustaining income.

hit refresh

Creating another source of income can, and should, be fun. The more you enjoy what you're doing, the easier it will be to do it. Are you a computer programmer with a penchant for soccer? There are so many ways to spin that, it makes me dizzy! For instance, retail sporting goods, coaching, freelance writing, fundraising…you get the picture!

What is your alternative earning power? I'm certain it's tied to what you love to do. So let's make a list of all of the things you *love* to do. It can be anything, like…

- sewing
- caring for children
- cooking
- baking
- exercising
- washing cars
- writing
- taking pictures
- fixing things
- cleaning
- caring for pets
- selling
- applying makeup

- decorating
- styling clothes
- organizing
- shooting videos
- styling hair
- painting
- coaching sports
- training
- shining shoes
- gardening
- listening to music

After creating your list, pick the top three and brainstorm with a friend about ways to turn those three things you love, into your "hustle."

Whatever you feel strongly attracted to, that is what you can creatively turn into extra money. The more you enjoy your side job, the more money you will make! If you're not careful, it may even become your full-time job!

talk to me...

What is your side gig? Do you have more than one?

Has your 'hustle' helped you at all during downturns in our economy?

Write and tell me about it!

@CharStallings
facebook.com/iwishbook

chapter 18
identity theft – be vigilant

Identity theft and electronic fraud is rampant and it can screw up your life. Our society and our lives are so driven by the internet and electronic money movement. It's not just a matter of who you allow into your home or who you give access to your personal information. Even taking the most extreme precautions doesn't guarantee you won't be a victim.

Several years ago, someone stole my purse. I reported it to the bank, closed my accounts and cancelled my credit cards. I didn't report my driver's license as stolen, I just requested a replacement. About four weeks later, the FBI showed up at my office with pictures asking me if I was the woman in the photos trying to withdraw money from an ATM. Two weeks later, I got a call from a local bank, they said there was a woman in the drive-up with my driver's license claiming to be me and trying to cash a stolen check drawn on their bank. Needless to say I was furious. I explained the situation and went to the bank to sign an affidavit of fraud. This woman had wreaked havoc on my life just with my driver's license.

I thought that was my one and only bout with fraud, but I was wrong. More recently, a joint account that my husband and I used for household expenses was hacked. We discovered the problem just as were about to leave for vacation. Packed and ready to go, my husband went online to check our balance and pay a bill before we headed to the airport. "Why did you pay the electricity bill four times?" he asked me. "I didn't, that would be a stupid thing to do," I said. We looked closely at the account and realized someone had paid other people's electricity bills from our account. Those transactions totaled several thousand dollars. Neither of us had lost or misplaced our cards, or bank checks – we were victims of online fraud. Thankfully we discovered this before leaving for our trip, and we were able to notify the bank. They refunded all of our money, and set up several alerts on the account to prevent this from happening again.

Even taking the most extreme precautions doesn't guarantee you won't be a victim.

Speaking of fraud, about a year ago close friend received a visit at their home by FBI Agents. It turns out someone had assumed their identity in a state that my friend had not been a resident of for at least 10 years. I can't begin to tell you how much of a problem this was for my friend. ◆

lesson

Carefully review all bank and credit cards statements, daily transactions and credit reports to guard against hacking, fraudulent activity and identity theft.

hit refresh

Chances are you know someone this has happened to or it may have happened to you. There are so many ways for your information to become compromised, so it's more important than ever to take all necessary precautions to guard against this!

Following are 5 steps I recommend to safeguard against fraud:

1. Make sure that you're checking your bank statements on a regular basis.
2. Change your passwords frequently.
3. Buy a shredder, and shred all documents and personal information with sensitive data such as your account number, social security number etc., *don't just throw it away.*
4. Make sure that your mail is secure when you are not home to pick it up.
5. Be cautious when giving out your credit card numbers online, via fax or by telephone.
6. You can also pay for the convenience of a company that watches your accounts for possible fraud. If a breach occurs, they will contact you but you will still need to manage the corrective action that is needed to resolve the problem. Do a Google search to research companies that provide this service.

If you are the victim of identity theft, here are 4 steps the Federal Trade Commission (FTC) says you should take immediately.

1. Place a fraud alert on your credit reports, and review your credit reports.

Fraud alerts can help prevent an identity thief from opening any more accounts in your name. Contact the toll-free fraud number of any of the three consumer reporting companies below to place a fraud alert on your credit report. You only need to contact one of the three companies to place an alert. The company you call is required to contact the other two, which will place an alert on their versions of your report, too.

TransUnion:
1-800-680-7289;
www.transunion.com;
Fraud Victim Assistance Division,
P.O. Box 6790,
Fullerton, CA 92834-6790

Equifax:
1-800-525-6285;
www.equifax.com;
P.O. Box 740241,
Atlanta, GA 30374-0241

Experian:
1-888-EXPERIAN (397-3742);
www.experian.com;
P.O. Box 9554,
Allen, TX 75013

2. Close the accounts that you know, or believe, have been tampered with or opened fraudulently.

Call and speak with someone in the security or fraud department of each company. Follow up in writing, and include copies (NOT originals) of supporting documents. It's important to notify credit card companies and banks in writing. Send your letters by certified mail, return receipt requested, so you can document what the company received and when.

3. File a complaint with the Federal Trade Commission.

Use the online complaint form; or call the

FTC's Identity Theft Hotline, at

1-877-ID-THEFT (438-4338);

TTY: 1-866-653-4261;

or write

Identity Theft Clearinghouse,

Federal Trade Commission,

600 Pennsylvania Avenue, NW,

Washington, DC 20580.

By sharing your identity theft complaint with the FTC, you will provide important information that can help law enforcement officials across the nation track down identity thieves and stop them.

4. File a report with your local police or the police in the community where the identity theft took place.

Call your local police department and tell them that you want to file a report about your identity theft. Ask them if you can file the report in person. If you cannot, ask if you can file a report over the Internet or telephone.

talk to me...

Have you experienced online fraud or identity theft?

How do you guard against it these days?

I'm curious about how careful people really are. Write and tell me about the steps that you take to stay secure.

@CharStallings
facebook.com/iwishbook

chapter 19
money lessons for kids

I wish someone had told me that there really are lots of ways to integrate money lessons into everyday life when you are teaching kids. The relationship that we model with money and the lessons that we teach our children, directly affect the kind of financial lives they will lead as adults.

In my case, I am very thankful for those adults (including my mom, Aunt Bernice, Pastor & Mrs. Jenkins, and Miss Hunter) who took the time to teach me the role that money played in my life, and the importance of managing it responsibly. The money lessons they taught me seemed to always center on one (or all) of these questions:

- Why did I need this money?
- Where would the money come from (for a project or purchase)?
- When did I need to have the money?
- How was I going to replace any money that was borrowed or pulled from savings?

Despite straying from these core money lessons (and questions) at certain points in my life, they stuck with me. When I think back, it was because of what had been drilled into me, that I could raise money as a Junior in high school to pay for a trip to Europe, and to save money for my bumble-bee car when I was in college. These lessons served me well.

Certain lessons felt like a "Rite of Passage", like the day my mother sat down with me and my siblings and showed us our life insurance policies. She explained what the policies would pay out if we were to die, and she showed us the monthly premiums. This was really exciting to me because I got to start paying my own $6 premium each month! I started working when I was 14, so I had cashflow, this $6 payment was going to be a breeze. I was proud as a peacock, you couldn't tell me I wasn't all grown up!

As a young grade school student, I remember my mother also made sure that each of us had a savings account through the local bank. On a designated day each week or month, we were allowed to bring money to school. We'd fill out our envelopes and our teachers would collect them. Once or twice each school year, we'd take a field trip to downtown Minneapolis to the old Farmers & Mechanics Bank to make our deposits in person. I remember this continuing for several years, until I suspect, it became too costly.

Now, as parents of a soon-to-be high school freshman, my husband and I have had to force ourselves to think about what we're teaching our daughter about money, and how we're teaching her. I'm in a better financial position in life than I was when I was a child and to be honest, I just want to buy my daughter stuff! I realized recently that we were not talking about money in a way that weaves its management into our everyday lives, nor were we exposing her to important money lessons. ◆

lesson

Regardless of your present financial situation, as a parent you cannot be lulled into a false sense of expecting that your kids will "figure it out." You have to teach them!!

hit refresh

Tie the practice of saving and spending money into the daily lives of your children instead of waiting for birthdays or holidays. Here are a few ways to expose your kids to saving money and money management. These are just a starting place, expand on them with your own ideas.

1. Let your children pick out something big that they want and help them plan to save in order to buy it.

2. If they have a list of items they want, tell them how much is available, and require that they spend the money on paper first, before you ever leave the house.

3. Let them screw-up. Allow them to make an unwise or frivolous purchase that requires all of their money. Then discuss how they felt when they were out of money.

4. Help your children explore ways to earn money.

5. Open a bank account for your children and take them to the bank or credit union to deposit their money.

6. Help your children start a savings program based on their allowances. Have them save $1 a week based on their age and with them, monitor their interest earned. You can also say, "I'm going to match a part of that." This creates an incentive for them to learn to save and later on

in life, an awareness of the value their employers play in matching contributions to their retirement plans.

Here are a few good websites to help you help your child(ren) get a strong start in being money smart. There are also numerous blog posts and online articles with great tips as well, search those out as well.

Count My Beanz
http://countmybeanz.com/

Three Jars
http://www.threejars.com/home

The Mint
www.themint.org

 talk to me...

What are some ways that you are helping your child get a strong start on being money smart?

How did your parents help you?

Care to share? I'd like to know!

@CharStallings
facebook.com/iwishbook

chapter 20
save for tuition *now*

Several years ago, a friend asked me how she could come up with the money to pay for her 16-year-old daughter's college education. "Well, you could buy Powerball tickets every week and pray that you win," I said, kind of half under my breath and half chuckling. Obviously she didn't think it was a laughing matter. With her right index finger swooshing through the air and her meanest 'evil eye' scowl she said, "Look, I know I'm behind the 8-ball on this one, okay?! I've been beating myself up for not saving when she was younger. When I did try to start putting money aside, I knew it wasn't nearly enough and I wasn't consistent. Now college is around the corner, and I'm worried. What can we do?"

I assured her that I understood the urgency she felt and that she wasn't alone because many other parents had the same anxiety. I wanted her to focus on the fact that she did have some time *and* she had options. "Hey, no more should've, would've, could've – let it go!" I said. "Let's focus on what you do have, and that's two full years before she sets foot on a college campus. You also have lots of different approaches for tackling the future tuition bills. The fact that you're talking about it is a good thing. Let's start right now putting our heads together to figure this out."

Sidebar: If you wait until your son or daughter is in their teens to start saving for college, it will take a lot more work on your part, *and* theirs, to get them there. With the rising cost of tuition, it's a great idea to start saving early (trust me, at conception isn't too early). This way, you can create a growing account that really eases the way for funding your child's education.

When we ran the numbers for my friend, it turned out that even with an aggressive savings plan, it was still going to be a struggle to handle the first few years of the most modest tuition expenses. As a result, she and her daughter decided to explore less expensive, local college options and applied for financial aid, grants, and scholarships. Her daughter started out at a community college, working part-time to help pay the bills, and after a couple years, she was accepted at a local university. When she graduated she landed a good job, and like many other college students, she had a sizeable student loan tab. The last time I talked to her, she was working hard to pay off those bills. The last time I talked to her mom, she said,

If you wait until your son or daughter is in their teens to start saving for college, it will take a lot more work on your part, and theirs, to get them there.

"I wish someone had told me that waiting until your child is older to start saving for college, makes paying for college much harder later on." ◆

lesson

Saving money for college *early* on is one of the best things you can do for you and your child. Even if you can only save a small amount each month, *save it!*

hit refresh

"Depending on the number of children you have, paying for college is the most expensive event outside of paying for retirement," says Fred Amrein, ChFC® and principal of Amrein Financial in Wynnewood, Pa. Many experts agree that the total price of paying for college can be decreased by making smart decisions. So it benefits parents (or parents-to-be) to start planning for this expense sooner rather than later.

Let's look at a couple scenarios to understand some of the ways you can save or pay for college for your kid(s).

Scenario #1: Your children are young, or maybe you don't have kids now, but you plan to in the future. You may even have plans of a first, or advanced, degree for yourself!

Today there are more options than ever before to save for college. Many people have used traditional investments like savings accounts, taxable investment accounts, annuities, and U.S. Savings Bonds. And now, newer investment choices are available including Coverdell education savings accounts, and my favorite (that I'll elaborate on), Section 529 college savings programs.

A 529 Plan is an education savings plan operated by a state or educational institution designed to help families set aside funds for future college costs.

It is named after Section 529 of the Internal Revenue Code which created these types of savings plans in 1996. You deposit after-tax money into the 529 account and it grows tax-deferred. When money is distributed from the account to pay for qualified higher education expenses, it comes out federally tax-free.

Some of the key benefits of 529's include:

- Federal tax benefits
- State tax benefits
- Account owner retains control
- Low maintenance
- Simple tax reporting
- Flexibility
- Substantial deposits allowed

As you research 529's, be sure to check out one of the best and most comprehensive sites I know of, www.savingforcollege.com. And do yourself a favor, make an appointment with a financial adviser to discuss your situation and to get help determining how a 529 (or other college savings strategies) will benefit you.

Scenario #2: You find yourself in my friend's shoes with two or three years before the first day of college.

I agree with the 5-step approach outlined below that www.360financialliteracy. org recommends for these situations.

First, help your child investigate schools that provide a good value. Some less expensive state universities and second-tier private colleges may offer better programs than their more expensive private counterparts. Think creatively.

Second, learn all you can about financial aid. Do a dry run through the federal government's financial aid application to determine whether your child is likely to qualify for financial aid, and, if so, for how much.

Third, start investigating potential scholarships. There are a number of websites where your child can type in his or her interests, abilities, and goals to obtain a list of relevant scholarships. (Speaking of scholarships, www.yourscholarshipcoach.com consults students and their parents on how to attend college on other people's money.)

Fourth, examine any current financial resources that you can draw on for the early college bills. Do you have savings accounts, stocks, mutual funds, or cash value life insurance? Can you pay a portion of the tuition bills from current income? Can you increase the family income by getting a second job or having a previously stay-at-home spouse return to the work force?

Finally, you'll need to start earmarking a portion of your current income for college bills that won't come due until four or five years, when your child is a junior or senior in college.

Another sidebar: Can your son or daughter hold some of the financial responsibility for their college years? My husband and I had a combination of scholarships, grants and financial aid. I also worked every year that I was in school to pay tuition and fees. When it's time for our daughter to go to college, I think she will appreciate it more, and apply herself a bit more, if she has some skin in the game, but that's just me. Yet it doesn't mean I'm not already saving now! What about you?

talk to me...

How have you managed to save money for your child's education?

If you didn't start early, what other options did you use to pay for college?

Will your child be involved in funding their college bills?

I'm curious and interested?

@CharStallings
facebook.com/iwishbook

chapter 21
how big was your tax refund?

When you get a tax refund check that could mean you've given the federal government an interest free loan for at least a year. You could be overwithholding (having too much withheld from your paycheck). Do you think the IRS would reciprocate and give you a big fat loan every year? Not hardly! In fact, they impose stiff penalties and fees if you don't file or pay on time. One thing you may want to look into is the number of withholdings entered on your W-4. Overwithholding and underwithholding (not having enough withheld which results in owing the IRS) are both bad. The best scenario is to have just enough withheld so that the amount will come as close as possible to your actual tax liability for the year.

I used to celebrate when I found out I had a nice, big tax refund check coming. I would plan those purchases with my newfound wealth in exacting detail, while watching the mailbox each day to get my money and run! Several years later, I read an enlightening magazine article that said to go back and look at what you are having deducted from your paycheck on a regular basis.

What a surprise! I discovered that I was overpaying because of the number of withholdings I had listed. I hadn't taken the time to review my W-4 each year, even after I got married.

Take a look at what you paid in taxes in the last three years. Have your circumstances changed much since then? Have you been receiving tax refunds? This is a sign that you may need to review the number of withholdings listed on your W-4. Contact your Human Resources or Benefits department to obtain a copy of your W-4 they have on file. It may be time to make some adjustments to this form. If you're confused about it all, make an appointment to sit down and talk with a tax expert. It will be money well spent since their advice could save you a great deal in the years to come. ◆

lesson

The best kind of refund check is to receive no check at all!

hit refresh

As highlighted in a recent article on www.turbotax.com, "The key to paying the right amount of tax is to update your W-4 regularly. Do this whenever you have a major personal life change or event. The goal is to reduce the potential for both a tax bill and a tax refund to zero, or close to it."

According to TurboTax, here are 5 of the most common life events that should make you re-visit your W-4 withholding.

1. You get a second job
2. Your spouse gets a job or changes jobs
3. You're unemployed part of the year
4. You get married…or divorced
5. You have a baby…or adopt one

So how do you adjust your W-4 withholding if you've had a life event or you've been overwithholding? As outlined by the IRS at http://www.irs.gov/Individuals/IRS-Withholding-Calculator, here's what you need to do.

Use the Withholding Calculator http://apps.irs.gov/app/withholdingcalculator/ to help you determine whether you need to give your employer a new Form W-4 to avoid having too much or too little Federal income tax withheld from your pay. You can use your results from the calculator to help fill out the form.

Tips for completing the Withholding Calculator:

- Have your most recent pay stubs handy.
- Have your most recent income tax return handy.
- Estimate values if necessary, remembering that the results can only be as accurate as the input you provide.

Then to change your withholding:

- Use your results from the calculator to help you complete a new Form W-4.
- Submit the completed Form to your employer.

talk to me...

Have you had any life events that required you to adjust your W-4?

Have you been underwithholding or overwithholding?

Have you re-visited your W-4 to ensure that the IRS is taking the right amount from your paycheck?

Tell me what the process was like.

@CharStallings
facebook.com/iwishbook

chapter 22
who's your beneficiary?

A will is an important and necessary document to have in place, but it doesn't dictate who's going to get your retirement assets. Retirement and life insurance assets are considered non-probate assets; they go directly to the person you have named as a beneficiary. Have you looked at those names lately?

A friend of mine married her high school sweetheart right after college. They had a beautiful home and wonderful children, but they grew apart over time and divorced after 17 years. Within a few years, her ex-husband remarried and started a new family. Wanting to make sure his kids were provided for, he updated his will.

As fate would have it, he suffered a fatal heart attack nine years later. When his estate was settled, the kids got his "stuff", which certainly held great sentimental value, but the "real stuff" was his 401k and life insurance policy. These had grown in value over time and were quite substantial. As it turned out, my friend's ex had never gone back and updated the beneficiaries on these accounts. Guess who received the bulk of his estate? You're absolutely right, his *first* wife. ◆

 lesson

It is vitally important to keep your beneficiary designations updated.

⟳hit refresh

The situation I described above happens all the time. Here's what you should do:

1. Call your company's human resource department, your broker or your insurance agent and ask them to mail you a copy of your beneficiary designation forms.
2. Ask them to send a new form as well in case you want to change these names.
3. Any life change such as marriage, divorce, births or deaths may affect your decision on naming a beneficiary.
4. If you list a minor child as the beneficiary, make sure you also name a guardian who can be trusted.
5. Consider any non-person entities you may choose to leave money to also.

If you've changed jobs, be sure to contact former employers with whom you have old retirement accounts to request copies of the beneficiary forms they have on file for you. Review and update if needed and make changes there as well.

talk to me...

Do you remember who you listed as a beneficiary on your retirement accounts?

If you maintain retirement accounts with former employers, have you gone back to them and updated those beneficiary designation forms?

Do you have a current will?

@CharStallings
facebook.com/iwishbook

chapter 23
playing it safe can hurt

Sometimes we make decisions based on the advice of someone who appeared to be an expert, or on information we've heard over the years (or over the water cooler), but never took the time to investigate. Maybe we heard, "safe is better than sorry" or "don't put your money in the risky stuff." While these are useful nuggets of wisdom, without proper information and knowledge on long-term investment principles, you could be missing out on the opportunity to build a significant retirement nest egg because of playing it "too safe."

When I first started investing in my company's 401k plan, I remember overhearing a discussion between two people who had been in the department much longer than me; in my book, they were pretty knowledgeable. One person told the other, "Put your money into something safe. Don't take the risk of losing it." So, thinking I had received a special insider trading tip, I decided to have all of my contributions and the company match allocated to the most conservative options available. When I looked at my next two quarterly statements, I was proud of my slow, steady growth.

On my one-year anniversary with the company, I had lunch with a few co-workers who both started at the company the same day I did. When our conversation turned to benefits and our retirement accounts, I learned that I was behind the eight-ball. I put my fork down, sat back in my chair and listened. My colleagues talked about how much their 401k's had grown because they had diversified their investments, and also because they purposely chose to allocate dollars to some of the more aggressive options in the retirement plan offering. As I leaned forward in my chair, I wanted to kick myself because I didn't know about any of this. I was naïve and I didn't make good choices. The biggest mistake was that I didn't ask questions. "I wish we would've had this discussion a year ago," I thought to myself.

That day I learned a lot of lessons. One lesson was about inflation risk—investing too conservatively, it can result in investment returns not keeping pace with, or outpacing inflation. That was one of the reasons I wrote this book, to bring this to your attention, so you don't make the same mistakes I did.

Prior to that lunch, I had been excited about my "Steady-Eddy" nominal returns, but I learned I was woefully behind because of my "play it safe" mentality. I didn't understand the concept of time, and how I could afford to be more aggressive in my investment approach because I had a long-time horizon until reaching my retirement goal. ◆

The most conservative investments aren't necessarily the only ones you should own.

hit refresh

Look at where you're putting your money inside your 401k, 403b or IRA. Is it in the most conservative choice? If so, ask yourself why you've done this. If you are nearing or in retirement this could be a smart move to preserve your principle. If, however, you have a long time before you reach the goal you have for this money (seven or more years away…retirement, education etc.), then maybe it's worthwhile to work with a financial adviser who can help you understand the other options you have, and how they might effect your portfolio performance.

Each of us has a different degree of comfort or nervousness with the amount of fluctuation or stability built into our investment portfolio. Understanding your personal risk tolerance before making an investment is a smart step. Consult a financial adviser to help you better understand how you feel about fluctuations in your portfolio. Had I done this at that time, I would have realized there were lots of options that would help me maximize my investment returns, and that I could create a balance between conservative and aggressive instruments.

talk to me...

Do you know your risk tolerance?

What level of risk are you taking today?

I'm interested in your thoughts.

@CharStallings
facebook.com/iwishbook

chapter 24
understand what you invest in

Know what you're buying. "Duh, that's seems pretty obvious Charlotte, why are you making this statement?" I'm saying it because I've witnessed first-hand what happens when people don't fully understand what they're investing their hard-earned money in. More often than not, they do so because they don't want to look unintelligent in front of friends, family, co-workers, or their financial advisers. If you don't understand the company you're putting your money into, or the investment structure being used, do yourself a favor and keep the money in your pocket or wherever it is right now.

As a first step to understanding what you're investing in, consider the companies or businesses you frequent, such as your grocer or pharmacy. And don't forget about the products and services that you can't (or don't want to) live without, like shampoos or dry cleaning? Are any of these publicly traded companies that you can invest in, either by purchasing shares directly, or through buying shares in a mutual fund? These could be great options to consider because you're not just familiar with these goods and services, you use them on a regular basis.

In your research (and yes you should do your own research, don't simply rely on others' recommendations), think about why you are buying into this company. What do they do? What's on the horizon for them? What are their growth strategies? Learn everything you can about them. This can be fun and interesting as you become fully versed in their history, goals and progress. If you need to call them up and ask them some questions, go ahead. Go visit if you need to. Read, read, read! Read and ask questions until you don't have any more questions. And by all means, don't invest until you're completely informed.

If you don't understand, do yourself a favor and keep the money in your pocket.

It was very early in my investment career and my husband and I were saving money for a house. I was responsible for putting our down payment money into a suitable investment. I chose a large-cap stock mutual fund: a great long-term investment. I thought I understood this mutual fund, but I didn't.

Within a couple of years we found a house that we wanted and I went to withdraw our down-payment. The market was down and since our mutual funds held a variety of stocks and that were subject to market fluctuations, I found our value had declined. In my mind, and especially in my husband's mind, that was *not* the way it was supposed to work! The reality is that I didn't do my homework. I didn't ask enough questions to understand how this investment would perform in certain market conditions, nor did I understand that this was probably not the best vehicle for our short- to medium-term timeframe. Let's just say I completely screwed up on dotting *i*'s and crossing *t*'s. ◆

lesson

If you're considering a particular investment like a stock, bond, mutual fund or Real Estate Investment Trust (REIT), ask yourself, "What do I know about this?

hit refresh

If you are considering a particular investment like a stock, bond, mutual fund or Real Estate Investment Trust (REIT), ask yourself, "What do I know about this?" Your answer should be more than where the company is headquartered or what the particular share price is. You are looking for information about this company's position within its industry. For instance:

- Major holdings or other businesses.
- How do they make money?
- What are the strengths of the company leaders?
- What are trends in the industry over five, 10 and 20 years?
- What sort of cash reserves does the company have?

If it's a mutual fund, managed account or annuity, do you know:

- About the fees you'll pay?
- How much risk/fluctuation the investment may have annually?
- What the underlying investments are?
- What happens if you redeem money within a certain time?
- Anything about the team managing the assets?

Taking the time to conduct proper due diligence (research upfront) can mean the difference between significant earnings and a loss. Doing some degree of research also equips you to have a meaningful discussion with a financial adviser, who is an expert on these matters. You don't have to try to navigate this alone, in fact, I don't advise that you do. Do what you can to be informed and partner with a professional who can help you understand the investment options that meet your goals, timeframe, tax bracket and risk tolerance.

Here are a few helpful sites to help you learn more about investments you may be considering:

The Street
www.thestreet.com

The Motley Fool
www.fool.com

Investopedia
www.investopedia.com

Investor Guide
www.investorguide.com

The Wall Street Journal
Online.wsj.com

talk to me...

Where do you go to learn more about investments?

What do you do differently now, in your research, than you did several years ago?

Do you work with a financial adviser to help you understand and select investments?

I'd like to hear.

@CharStallings
facebook.com/iwishbook

conclusion
get started now!

My husband and I had known each other six and a half years before we shared our financial information with one another. While we were both born and raised in the Midwest, we came from very different places relative to our perspective on life and money. Ron was the youngest of three children; he loved new, shiny and expensive things. Buy first; figure out how to pay for it later was his mantra. I was the oldest of five children and had been the bossy family caretaker (think Thelma from Good Times). In my heart I was a penny-pinching, spend-thrift, but on paydays, I lost myself at the mall and my favorite boutiques. Do you see how our differences created a perfect backdrop for the financial challenges that were sure to come?

Today we have Glen Beecham to thank for our financial freedom. Glen held a series of financial seminars at our church, and although we were reluctant to attend at first (because people would think we had money problems…which we did), we became regular attendees. The next topic on the schedule was 'Planned Spending'; we were on the front row.

Glen talked about putting cash into envelopes to help curb spending (our first introduction to The Envelope System) as well as other common sense ideas that could help people manage their money better. On the way home in the car, my husband and I didn't speak about what we heard and we didn't discuss it when we got home either. Finally, over the weekend, I got up my courage and asked him what he thought about the seminar. "Maybe we should ask Glen over and see if he can help us," my husband said.

When Glen arrived at our home, he asked us to gather every credit card and installment loan bill we had and lay them out, end-to-end, on the table. My heart was beating so fast I thought it would jump out of my chest as I revealed all 20 of the bills I had racked up over the years. Yep, 20! With my head down and eyes closed, I anxiously bit my lip and held my breath in anticipation of a big groan (followed by a few choice words) I expected to hear from my husband. I also expected to hear Glen's feet shuffling, no.....running to the door to get away from this impossible situation. But to my surprise, and relief, neither happened. There were no deep breaths, neck rolls, shifting eyes, or finger pointing. Glen simply said, "Good, now that everything is *out on the table*, in the open, we know exactly what we're working with. I'm here to help, not condemn, so let's get started!" That was one of the most liberating and productive meetings I had ever had. Glen encouraged us to establish a joint account to handle our cash flow, and he shared tips on how we could became completely accountable to one another for our spending.

Our differences created a perfect backdrop for the financial challenges that were sure to come.

I'd love to tell you this process was "easy breezy" as one of my nieces says, but it wasn't! It was one of the hardest things I've ever had to work through. We'd come home from work on Friday nights and watch Cheers on television instead of going out for a movie and dinner. Guests were disappointed when the parties at our house got less fancy. "If that's the food you're serving I'm going home to eat," said one family member. When we needed a new car, my husband bought an old van from his brother and we slid around town with bad brakes and bald tires until we could finally trade it in for a used Taurus station wagon (yes, I drove a station wagon back in the day!)

But things got better. We used the envelopes, we developed a spending plan, we saved money and we eventually got our first Lexus, only 3-years-old at the time. We talked about our money, and planned out our purchases. We stashed our cash in the right investments, and started putting money aside for our daughter's college education. And to top it all off, we survived several layoffs, a tropical storm and a few hurricanes as well! ◆

lesson

I wish someone had told me that getting started is the hardest part to managing your money effectively. But until you start, you can't turn things around in your financial life.

So how do you get started?

hit refresh

Yes, getting started is the hardest part, so don't try to tackle all of this at once. There are plenty of ideas in this book, and all you need to do is start on *one* of them. Take it one chapter at a time or chose a category that will help you the most.

As a re-cap, here are some topics that I've touched on in this book. What resonates with you? Where do you want to start?

- Talking about money - with family, friends, roommates, spouse, etc.
- Building cash reserves.
- Developing positive, wise, spending habits.
- Budgeting and paying bills.
- Fraud and identity theft

Once you've decided what you want to work on, formulate a goal around it and write it down in a positive sense, with lots of detail. You also want to make your goal SMART, which is Specific, Measurable, Achievable, Realistic and Time-sensitive. And then talk about it! Tell your spouse, your friends, you neighbors and your family about those goals. It will make you accountable and you'll get lots of encouragement.

And once you achieve one goal, then go on to the next one….

I hope you'll enjoy this book for years to come and use it to develop careful spending and good saving habits. Together, with just a bit of plain common sense, we can all achieve a level of prosperity that brings satisfaction and financial freedom.

talk to me...

Did you read something in these pages that will help you or a family member?

How will you apply what you've learned to your life?

I really do want to know!

@CharStallings
facebook.com/iwishbook

Please tell your friends, family members,
and colleagues about
I Wish Someone Had Told Me!

Purchases can be made online at
www.charlottestallings.com/charlotte-stallings-book/

If you would like Charlotte to speak
at your upcoming event, complete the form at
www.charlottestallings.com/contact/
or send an email to
charlotte@charlottestallings.com.

notes

notes

Made in the USA
Charleston, SC
17 March 2013